Especia

....
From

....
Date

....

Written and compiled by Leah Slawson.

ISBN 978-1-61626-429-1

Published by Barbour Publishing, Inc., P.O. Box 719, Uhrichsville, Ohio 44683, www.barbourbooks.com

Our mission is to publish and distribute inspirational products offering exceptional value and biblical encouragement to the masses.

Printed in China.

101 Reasons You're Special

BARBOUR
PUBLISHING

1.

You hold a very important place in my heart.

Promise me you'll always remember:
you're braver than you believe,
and stronger than you seem,
and smarter than you think.

<small>Christopher Robin to Winnie the Pooh</small>

2.

You have a generous spirit,
sharing yourself with those around you.

Since you get more joy out of giving joy to others,
you should put a good deal of thought
into the happiness that you are able to give.

ELEANOR ROOSEVELT

3.

You inspire others to keep their eyes
on the goal but their feet on the ground.

Don't ask what the world needs.
Ask what makes you come alive, and go do it.
Because what the world needs
is people who have come alive.

HOWARD THURMAN

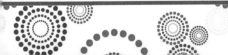

A thief comes only to rob, kill, and destroy.
I came so that everyone would have life,
and have it in its fullest.

JOHN 10:10 CEV

4.

You are steady and solid,
loyal and loving,
responsible and reliable.

5.

You listen without judgment,
counsel when asked,
and give without expectation.

Friendship is born at that moment
when one person says to another,
"What! You, too? I thought I was the only one!"

C. S. LEWIS

6.

You are the object of divine affection;
the apple of His eye.

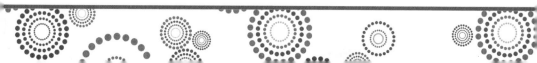

Who loves not a false imagining,
an unreal character in us;
but looking through all the rubbish of our imperfections,
loves in us the divine ideal of our natures—
not the man that we are, but the angel that we may be.

ALFRED, LORD TENNYSON

7.

You have a laugh like no one else's.
It is contagious.

Laughter is the sun that drives
winter from the human face.

VICTOR HUGO

You offer hugs and handshakes,
the grace of friendship.

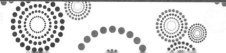

Think where man's glory most begins and ends,
And say my glory was I had such friends.

WILLIAM BUTLER YEATS

9.

You are not afraid of change in yourself or others.
You accept life's transitions
and gracefully move through them.

1e.

You finish what you start.
You go the whole way.
You are willing to be dependable
even when it is costly.
You get the job done!

*"There is no greater love than to
lay down one's life for one's friends."*

John 15:13 NLT

11.

Your eyes see things your way.
Your perspective is unique and inspiring.

The greatest good you can do for another is not just to share your riches, but to reveal to him his own.

BENJAMIN DISRAELI

12.

You star in many roles. . .friend, neighbor, parent,
child, sibling, cousin, and colleague.
You give your best.

It is one of the blessings of old friends that
you can afford to be stupid with them.

RALPH WALDO EMERSON

113.

You create the feeling of home wherever you are.

14.

You spur others on to live the truth,
be their best, push harder, and go deeper.

Optimism is the faith that leads to achievement.
Nothing can be done without hope and confidence.

HELEN KELLER

15.

You live in the present,
appreciating the moment you have been given.

A tree is known by its fruit; a man by his deeds.
A good deed is never lost; he who sows courtesy reaps
friendship, and he who plants kindness gathers love.

St. Basil

16.

You are God's child, made in His image, and fitted for good works to glorify Him.

Above all, love each other deeply,
because love covers over a multitude of sins.
Offer hospitality to one another without grumbling.

1 PETER 4:8–9 NIV

17.

Others are drawn to you in the same way they are to a warm fire on a chilly night.

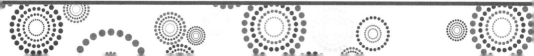

Where there is room in the heart,
there is room in the house.

DANISH PROVERB

18.

You are strong, for God strengthens His people.
You are wonderful, made by a God
who does wonders.

He sends a cross,
but He also sends the strength to bear it.

LEO TOLSTOY

19.

You are not only smart, you're wise,
learning from experience and remaining teachable.

Wise men speak because they have something to say;
Fools because they have to say something.

PLATO

20.

You start the conversation.
You extend your hand.
You get the ball rolling.

Be kind and compassionate to one another,
forgiving each other, just as in Christ God forgave you.

EPHESIANS 4:32 NIV

21.

You put others first and self-interest aside.

22.

You are like still water and soft,
floating clouds, able to calm and soothe
a troubled soul that comes to you.

23.

You tell the truth and
hold those you love accountable.

Optimist: Person who travels on nothing
from nowhere to happiness.

MARK TWAIN

24.

You find the best in others,
knowing their past, accepting their present,
and believing in their potential.

God created a marvelous,
incredibly detailed work in you.

PAMELA MCQUADE

25.

You experience and express faith
in your own unique way.
Others learn more of God by being with you.

26.

When I unravel,
you are there to sew me up again.

The best portion of a good man's life is his little,
nameless, unremembered acts of kindness and of love.

WILLIAM WORDSWORTH

27.

Your listening is like a filter.
When I am done pouring out my troubles,
I've captured what is needed to move forward
and can discard the rest.

A kind heart is a fountain of gladness,
making everything in its vicinity freshen into smiles.

WASHINGTON IRVING

*Friend, you have no idea how good
your love makes me feel,
doubly so when I see your hospitality to fellow believers.*

PHILEMON 1:7 MSG

28.

You are willing to be silent with me.
You can be comfortable with space between us.

I like your silence,
it the more shows off your wonder.

WILLIAM SHAKESPEARE

29.

Your presence is a comforting fragrance
like fresh-baked cookies or homemade soup.

Like each raindrop watering the earth,
you are a necessary part of the whole.

We are all alike on the inside.

MARK TWAIN

31.

You live a life of sweet contentment.

32.

You give thanks from a humble heart.
You know your life and all of
its blessings are a gift.

Gratitude is not only the greatest of virtues,
but the parent of all the others.

Marcus Tullius Cicero

33.

You are able to grow in the soil
you've been planted in, despite the droughts,
winds, and storms that have come your way.

Let no one ever come to you without leaving better and happier. Be the living expression of kindness in your face, kindness in your eyes, kindness in your smile.

MOTHER TERESA

34.

You ask little in return
for hospitality and friendship.
You seem to get pleasure only in giving.

So let's not allow ourselves to get fatigued doing good. At the right time we will harvest a good crop if we don't give up, or quit. Right now, therefore, every time we get the chance, let us work for the benefit of all, starting with the people closest to us in the community of faith.

GALATIANS 6:9–10 MSG

35.

Your smile says,
"You are wanted here.
Welcome. Come on in."

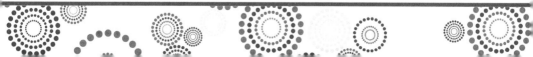

There are men whose presence
infuses trust and reverence.

T. S. ELIOT

36.

You enjoy surprises,
both giving them and receiving them.

37.

You are a treasured work of art, fashioned with exquisite beauty, a one-of-a-kind piece.

The strongest influences in my life and my work are always whomever I love. Whomever I love and am with most of the time, or whomever I remember most vividly.
I think that's true of everyone, don't you?

TENNESSEE WILLIAMS

38.

You lift the weight of my burden
and help me carry my load. Thank you.

39.

You add sugar and spice to the lives
of everyone around you.

40.

You stand up for what you believe.

You do the right thing even when it is not popular.

It is curious—curious that physical courage should be so common in the world, and moral courage so rare.

MARK TWAIN

Be on your guard; stand firm in the faith;
be courageous; be strong.

1 CORINTHIANS 16:13 NIV

41.

You don't have to have your own way.
You let others go first and
give them the biggest piece.

42.

You take time to pet dogs and notice children
and open the door for strangers.

43.

You are like an anchor, willing to disappear and hold fast at the bottom to keep the rest of us afloat.

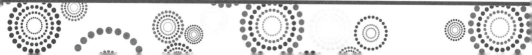

I am a success today because I had a friend who believed in me and I didn't have the heart to let him down.

ABRAHAM LINCOLN

44.

You have practiced.
You have worked hard and disciplined yourself
to be good at what you do.

45.

You are transparent.

Your life is like an open book for others to read,

learn from, and enjoy.

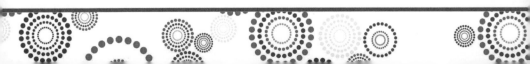

What do we live for;
if it is not to make life less difficult to each other?

T. S. ELIOT

46.

You keep cool in a crisis.
You don't panic at the first sign of trouble.

A peaceful man does more good than a learned one.

POPE JOHN XXIII

47.

You give yourself when people are demanding and difficult because you are needed and it is right to do so. Without reward and at cost to yourself, you lend your hand to others.

48.

You have learned to relinquish,
to let go of what you cannot control.

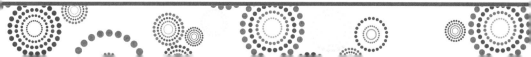

Brothers, I do not consider that I have made it my own.
But one thing I do: forgetting what lies behind and
straining forward to what lies ahead,
I press on toward the goal for the prize
of the upward call of God in Christ Jesus.

PHILIPPIANS 3:13–14 ESV

Far better is it to dare mighty things,
to win glorious triumphs,
even though checked by failure. . .
than to rank with those poor spirits
who neither enjoy much nor suffer much,
because they live in a gray twilight
that knows not victory nor defeat.

THEODORE ROOSEVELT

49.

You try; you take risks.

You have dared to do. Good for you!

50.

You have integrity.
What you see is what you get.
Authentic! Genuine! Bona fide!

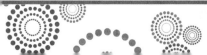

It is in our lives and not our
words that our religion must be read.

THOMAS JEFFERSON

51.

You live a life worthy of examination.
You are a good role model for others.

52.

You don't complain.

You don't criticize others.

You are positive, upbeat, and encouraging.

You use your words to lift others up.

I wanted to change the world.
But I have found that the only thing
one can be sure of changing is oneself.

ALDOUS HUXLEY

53.

You dig deep.
You are willing to ask yourself
the hard questions and allow yourself
to be transformed.

54.

You have an invisible life,
an inner self, made alive by God's spirit
to dwell with Him now and for all eternity.

Ordinary riches can be stolen, real riches cannot.
In your soul are infinitely precious things
that cannot be taken from you.

OSCAR WILDE

Don't store up treasures on earth! Moths and rust can destroy them, and thieves can break in and steal them. Instead, store up your treasures in heaven, where moths and rust cannot destroy them, and thieves cannot break in and steal them.

MATTHEW 6:19–20 CEV

55.

You are a lighthouse,
sending signals that offer safety
and point out danger at the same time.

56.

You pray.
The best gift you give those you love
is petitioning heaven for them.

57.

Your passions are uniquely yours to develop
and pursue and pass on to others.
You have gifts and creative ways to share those
gifts that no one else can duplicate.

Nothing great was ever achieved without enthusiasm.

RALPH WALDO EMERSON

58.

You find humor in the most ordinary things.
You make others laugh, and they relish in the fun.

59.

You have forgotten yesterday's mistakes and moved forward in the new mercy of the morning.

60.

You are a collection of all your life's experiences.
You have sorrows, triumphs, and trials you share
with others. You tell your stories
and pass along lessons to others.

The truth is always exciting.
Speak it, then. Life is dull without it.

PEARL S. BUCK

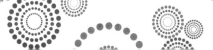

61.

You seek the truth, to know it, live it, speak it, and share it with others.

62.

You put feet to your prayers.
You walk your talk. You live out your calling.

*So we keep on praying for you,
asking our God to enable you to live a life worthy
of his call. May he give you the power to accomplish
all the good things your faith prompts you to do.*

2 THESSALONIANS 1:11 NLT

63.

You have been put in this place
at this time for a purpose.

Do not fear mistakes.
You will know failure.
Continue to reach out.

BENJAMIN FRANKLIN

64.

You have an adventurous spirit.
You are willing to take risks.
You don't let fear hold you back.

65.

You always want to learn something new.

Be not angry that you cannot make others
as you wish them to be,
since you cannot make yourself
as you wish to be.

Thomas à Kempis

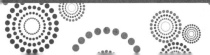

66.

You are patient with others,
knowing God is patient with you.

67.

You walk alongside your friends,
holding their hands or helping carry their load
of sorrow, easing the weight for them
by taking some of it yourself.

68.

You greet people with grace,
accepting them just as they are.

The pessimist sees difficulty in every opportunity.
The optimist sees opportunity in every difficulty.

WINSTON CHURCHILL

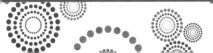

69.

You value beauty and order
and work to create it in the world around you.

*I will take pleasure in your laws
and remember your words. . . .
Help me to understand your teachings,
and I will think about your marvelous deeds.*

PSALM 119:16, 27 CEV

70.

You have purpose guiding your life,
meaning in your choices, fruit for your labor.

This is the true joy of life,
the being used up for a purpose recognized
by yourself as a mighty one.

GEORGE BERNARD SHAW

71.

You don't live in fear of people
nor do you live for their applause.
You live free for an audience of One.

72.

You honor others.

You don't show favoritism.

You respect people and treat them with dignity,

regardless of who they are.

Only those who respect the personality of others
can be of real use to them.

ALBERT SCHWEITZER

113.

You don't let worry pull and tear at you.
You don't fret, and you are not anxious.
You trust God, and His peace shows in your life.

74.

You don't dredge up the past,
remember others' mistakes,
hold grudges, or harbor bitterness.

You have enemies? Good.
That means you've stood up for something,
sometime in your life.

75.

You are a person of genuine conviction.
You have a moral compass guiding
your life and leading those around you.
You do the right thing.

God, the one and only—I'll wait as long as he says.
Everything I hope for comes from him, so why not?
He's solid rock under my feet, breathing room for my soul,
an impregnable castle: I'm set for life. My help and glory
are in God—granite-strength and safe-harbor-God—
So trust him absolutely, people; lay your lives on
the line for him. God is a safe place to be.

PSALM 62:5–8 MSG

76.

You have goals and dreams.
You believe in inspiration.
You have it yourself,
and you infuse it into others.

You aspire to great things?
Begin with little ones.

ST. AUGUSTINE

77.

You pay attention to the details.

You notice the little things.

You value the smallest gestures.

78.

You don't seek glory for yourself
but strive to make others successful.

Ninety-nine percent of the failures come from people who have the habit of making excuses.

GEORGE WASHINGTON CARVER

19.

You make things happen.
You don't make excuses.
You don't procrastinate.

So.

You trust people.
You are not naïve, and you have been disappointed,
but still you assume the best in others
and give each one a chance.

81.

You don't use people for your own purposes,
or step on them when they get in your way.
You revere other people and are careful with them.

Pray, and let God worry.

MARTIN LUTHER

82.

You know where to go when you get in trouble.
God is your Father. You rely on Him,
and He never lets you down.

Is anyone crying for help? God is listening,
ready to rescue you. If your heart is broken,
you'll find God right there; if you're kicked in the gut,
he'll help you catch your breath.
Disciples so often get into trouble;
still, God is there every time.

PSALM 34:17–19 MSG

Build me a son, O Lord,
who will be strong enough to know when he is weak,
and brave enough to face himself when he is afraid,
one who will be proud and unbending in honest defeat,
and humble and gentle in victory.

DOUGLAS MACARTHUR

83.

You prepare for what is coming.

You do your homework.

You are ready when it is time to go.

84.

You are not a complainer or a whiner.
Instead, you fill your speech with encouragement.

Remember not only to say the right thing
in the right place, but far more difficult still,
to leave unsaid the wrong thing
at the tempting moment.

BENJAMIN FRANKLIN

85.

You don't take yourself too seriously. . .
or anyone else, for that matter.

86.

You know that this world is not our home.
You live your life as a pilgrim on a journey.

Faith has to do with things that are not seen
and hope with things that are not at hand.

THOMAS AQUINAS

87.

You celebrate morning sunlight,
the color of fall leaves,
the song of a robin,
and the smell of fresh-cut grass.

88.

You are not jealous or controlling.
You give others room to make their own choices
and freedom to live their own lives.

Peace begins with a smile.

MOTHER TERESA

You tell the best stories!

"But he knows where I am going.
And when he tests me,
I will come out as pure as gold.
For I have stayed on God's paths;
I have followed his ways and not turned aside."

Job 23:10–11 NLT

Instruction does much,
but encouragement does everything.

90.

You call. You e-mail.

You write a note. You send a text.

Just at the right moment,

a word from you arrives.

91.

You are secure in who you are.
You will be yourself and let me be myself.

Be silly. Be honest. Be kind.

RALPH WALDO EMERSON

I am not afraid of storms,
for I am learning how to sail my ship.

Louisa May Alcott

92.

You know just the right times
to let your hair down and be crazy!

93.

You have creative power.
You have your own unique ideas to be expressed
in a way only you can say them.

I have been impressed with the urgency of doing.
Knowing is not enough; we must apply.
Being willing is not enough; we must do.

LEONARDO DA VINCI

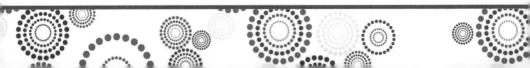

94.

You are a doer,
a you-can-count-on-me kind of person.
You don't just have an idea.
You have a plan of attack,
can gather an army,
and move out to make change.

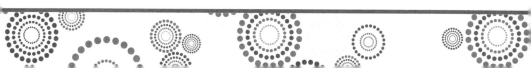

95.

You take your time. . .
to think. . .to speak. . .
to ponder. . .to listen. . .to act.

The greatest compliment that was ever paid me
was when one asked me what I thought,
and attended to my answer.

HENRY DAVID THOREAU

Whoever belittles his neighbor lacks sense,
but a man of understanding remains silent.

PROVERBS 11:12 ESV

96.

You value my thoughts.
You are careful with my feelings.
You are patient, and you listen well.

Give every man thy ear,
but few thy voice.

WILLIAM SHAKESPEARE

97.

You enjoy life and make anything fun.
If you are there, it's a party!
You make memories for those you love.

You have a compassionate heart.
You cry with others and look
for ways to soothe their pain.

If I can stop one heart from breaking,
I shall not live in vain.

EMILY DICKINSON

99.

Your smile is light,
and your laughter is music to those who love you.

100.

You are loyal.
Devotion is a hallmark of your character.
Once you commit, you are there to stay.

You have been my friend.
That in itself is a tremendous thing. . . .
After all, what's a life, anyway?
We're born, we live a little while, we die. . . .
By helping you, perhaps I was trying
to lift up my life a trifle.
Heaven knows anyone's life can stand a little of that.

CHARLOTTE TO WILBUR
FROM *CHARLOTTE'S WEB* BY E. B. WHITE

101.

You are a wonderful you!
There's no substitute for that.